PAUL WILSON

PENGUIN BOOKS

PENGUIN BOOKS

Published by the Penguin Group
Penguin Books Ltd, 27 Wrights Lane, London W8 5TZ, England
Penguin Putnam Inc., 375 Hudson Street, New York, New York 10014, USA
Penguin Books Australia Ltd, Ringwood, Victoria, Australia
Penguin Books Canada Ltd, 10 Alcorn Avenue, Toronto, Ontario, Canada M4V 3B2
Penguin Books (NZ) Ltd, Private Bag 102902, NSMC, Auckland, New Zealand

Penguin Books Ltd, Registered Offices: Harmondsworth, Middlesex, England

First published by Penguin Books Australia 1998
Published in Penguin Books 1999
1 3 5 7 9 10 8 6 4 2

Set in Bernhard Modern
Printed in England by William Clowes Ltd

What gives me pleasure

What a delight it is to suppose
there are hundreds of thousands of
people — maybe just like you —
who are discovering **the world is a
much more enjoyable place** than the
evening news would have us believe.

living happily ever after

ABOUT THE AUTHOR

Paul Wilson is known the world over as the 'guru of calm'. His first book, *The Calm Technique*, is considered one of the most influential in the genre. His second, the bestseller *Instant Calm*, has been translated into nineteen languages. His third major calm book, *Calm at Work*, is becoming even more popular.

However, his smallest work has won him the greatest acclaim. *The Little Book of Calm* has spent more than twelve months at the top of the bestseller lists. Now he has also written *The Little Book of Calm at Work*, and the calm continues to spread.

Feel free to contact the author or share your calm at www.calmcentre.com

For fifteen years now I have been researching and writing books on the topic of calm. From the outset, my belief was that feeling calm should not be a chore, an obligation or a program you have to adhere to. It should be a pleasure! Sheer, unadulterated, guilt-free pleasure.

Because, when you think about it, it's impossible to feel bad, or stressed, while you're *feeling good*.

So, over the years, I've taken note of the things that make people feel good. Now, I've listed a hundred or so of them — for your pleasure. They contain a little instruction, a lot of suggestion.

Let this book fall open to any page for the suggestion that will work best for you at this moment. Close your eyes, absorb it all, and *let your subconscious have a ball* with it.

Most importantly, don't take it too seriously — this is meant to be *fun*!

Conquer all workplace tensions with
Paul Wilson's complete work,
Calm at Work.

Go back

Relive one forgotten **joy** from your childhood. Carry that feeling with you all day.

---

happy memories • home cooking • peace

2

Indulge your fantasies

Fantasise about pleasurable
situations and **you're much better off**
than someone who stoically 'faces up
to the reality' of the mundane.

---

blue lagoons • charming princes • yachts

Give shoes the boot

Feel the relief when you kick off
your shoes and meander barefoot
across soft, damp grass.

---

tai chi • sunny parks • gardens

Face up to the heat

On a crisp winter's day, **feel** the midday sun as it warms your naked cheek and reminds you of **the simple pleasures** of life.

---

daylight saving • cloudless skies

Come September

Wonder at the unnatural **delight**
of your November lilies coming
into bloom in September.

---

wind chimes • *four leaf clover*

Smile strangely

Smile at a stranger, while making
no other effort to communicate,
and **enjoy the surprise**
it engenders.

---

good hair days • kindness • loyalty

Perfection

Imagine how good you feel
after completing a difficult task
and your boss says '**perfect**'.

---

trust • recognition • admiration

Go bananas

Find the pleasure in potassium foods, such as bananas, because they're associated with **feelings of wellbeing** and cheerfulness.

---

summer fruits • home-grown tomatoes

Head nowhere

Escape with a good friend,
a book of poetry,
and no destination
in mind.

---

sidewalk cafés • love letters • Keats

Q

Keep on living

Appreciate the statistical
beauty of the fact that the older
you get, the more your life
expectancy increases.

---

long life • young Elvis • perfect scores

Look about you

Life is infinitely more enriching
when you notice it. Observe and you
will **see the beauty.**

---

passion • wildlife • peace & quiet

Rub on a rose

Massage a little rose oil onto your
skin and **experience** its aphrodisiacal
as well as its mood-enhancing
properties.

---

floating • body moisturiser • patchouli

Go it alone

Luxuriate in the pleasure of your own company from time to time. **Be comfortable** with having nothing to do, and you will luxuriate all the more.

---

empty queues • total silence • creation

Make love

---

foreplay • backrubs • safe encounters

Look on the bright side

Invest the little extra effort it takes
to **be positive and optimistic** –
it pays off over and over again.

polka dots • lucky escapes • cheers

Share with a friend

Share your joys with those who are
close to you. Not only does this
enrich your experiences, it enriches
your relationships as well.

---

cuddling • old photographs • conversation

Dine out on the view

At least once in your life **savour** a
fresh garden salad, picked before your
very eyes, in Provence.

---

cashmere • camembert • snowy alps

Chill down

Imagine the pleasurable sensation of a cool cotton pillow-case on a hot, sultry night. (Just leave it in the refrigerator for fifteen minutes before retiring.)

---

al fresco • peach iced tea • opal

Hear nothing

Listen for the sound of your own
silence, and there you'll **find
perfect harmony.**

---

perfect quiet • whispered nothings

Confide in a cat

Find peace from even your most
trivial concerns, by unburdening
yourself to a pet:
not only are they great listeners,
they never judge.

---

good friends • quiet contentment

Turn back your eyes

Life is much more fulfilling
and uplifting when you choose
to look at it through a child's eyes.
How would a child see what
you're seeing?

---

butterflies • sea shells • teddy bears

Bear in mind your birthday

Celebrate your specialness
by buying yourself a particularly
desirable present on your special
day of the year.

---

silk lingerie • Versace • Bollinger

Remove your bra

Feel the relief that comes from shedding the garments that restrict you: your necktie, your bra ... everything.

---

good health • wellbeing • freedom

Fake it

Pretend **you're feeling on top of the world**, and guess how you'll be feeling.

---

ice-cream • lucky charms • flowers

In the dark with Claude

Discover the meaning of magic by venturing out into the night of the next full moon, with your headphones and Claude Debussy's *Clair de Lune* (or Beethoven's *Moonlight Sonata*).

falling stars • sunsets • gypsy violins

Turn on the heat

One of the cheapest, yet most
indulgent pleasures, is to simply
unwind in a steaming hot shower
after a day of intense activity.

---

incense • relaxation • thick towels

Get fresh

Seek it out, suck it in ... but get as much fresh air as your lungs will allow – all that oxygen will **elevate your mood** in no time.

---

ocean views • mountain air • white sand

Give

Give more love than you expect
to receive and **you will be
doubly rewarded.**

---

valentines • fair play • unlimited choice

Search for the upside

You will be pleasantly surprised
to learn how good life can be
by taking one simple step:
strive to **find the good** in all you
do and encounter.

---

success • fluffy clouds • ripe peaches

Payday

A fitting **reward** for a hard week of
effort ... and it all happens again
same time next week.

---

weekends • quitting time • credit balance

Give yourself permission

You can **make yourself feel wonderful** simply by making the decision to feel wonderful. Give yourself permission to **feel good** – right now – even if it is only for a short while.

---

breakthroughs • your last exam

Down a pleasure cocktail

Consume an uplifting cocktail
of juiced blackcurrants and apple,
blended with banana – all will help
to **elevate your mood**.

---

ginseng • figs • papaya • Guinness

Look heavenward

Gaze at the wonder and infiniteness
of space on a clear night. See
yourself for what you are: an integral
player in this grand spectacle.

---

happy landings • kites • hope

Let go

Take a moment – only a moment –
to experience what it's like to
feel totally uninhibited.

---

making love • powder snow • daydreams

Hands-free strip

Indulge in the visual sensuousness
as you and your partner sit naked,
untouching, and **appreciate**
one another.

---

romance • friendship • undemanding love

Have your wine salted

Unwind with a glass of fine wine
in a bath of mineral salts.
Sip the wine, **lose yourself**
in the bath.

---

solitude • sweet dreams • chardonnay

Discount the kilojoules

Melt a marshmallow into hot
drinking chocolate and
savour every naughty kilojoule –
it's important to **live dangerously**
every now and then.

---

passionfruit soufflé • *cappuccino*

Turn on your enemies

Whisper something positive and 'unnecessary' to a person you thought you disliked.

---

reunions • blessings • heart-to-hearts

Fill yourself with beans

Appreciate that **life is so rich** when
you approach it with enthusiasm.
Even the most mundane activity can
be enjoyed if approached this way.

---

endorphins • fresh mown grass

Challenge the mirror

Gaze deeply into a mirror and
**observe how beautiful you really
are** under your skin.

---

honesty · being alive · soft light

Stroke and amuse

Your subconscious is at its most
effective in helping you **feel good**
if it is stroked and amused as
opposed to bullied.

---

pleasant thoughts • silence • vacations

Love freely

And, sooner or later, you'll **get more than your share** in return.

---

soulmates • secret admirers • sharing

Bare your sole

Submit yourself to the pleasure
of having your feet rubbed (or do it
yourself). Rubbing the acupressure
points on your soles will **ease you
into a relaxed state.**

---

intimacy • kindliness • free spirits

Gorge yourself on beauty

Seek out beauty in life, not for
the stimulation, but for the sheer
pleasure of the experience.

Monet • wildflowers • dolphins • doves

Read about Jane

Read *Jane Eyre* again tonight and
fall asleep believing that **good really
does triumph.**

---

brides • faith • gripping stories

Burn incense

Enjoy the peace of the centuries by burning incense. It works on the psycho-neuro centre of the brain to help you **feel good**.

---

lavender • clear eyes • meditation

Pause for an endorphin

Rest peacefully after strenuous activity, and **revel** in the pleasurable benefits of all those endorphins.

---

peaceful moments • perfect health • bliss

Cultivate a carrot

Plant a dozen carrots in a window box, and **nurture** them till dinner. (Carrots aid in the production of a neurochemical that enhances your mood.)

---

yellow roses • Japanese gardens

Put your lips to an Italian

Savour a delicious lemon gelato
as you melt in the sun and **imagine
you're on Italy's Amalfi** coast
on a Sunday.

---

strawberries • Sambucca • Armani

Sleep on success

Make the most of those dreamy
moments before drifting off to sleep
after an event that **everyone
proclaims a success.**

---

safe & sound • carefree souls • sleep

Hurt your face

Laugh ... so hard that your face hurts.

---

good humour • winning smiles • grins

Enjoy the countdown

Pause to **appreciate** the last minute
of your labours ... before you
complete a long and arduous task.

Friday night • fresh sheets • holidays

Cheer up

Talk cheerful talk, choose cheerful
words, and you'll talk yourself
into believing **you can become
cheerful** before you know it.

---

laughter • applause • good fortune • sex

Taste the man go

Share a juicy ripe mango, sitting
naked in the tub. Many believe
mangoes are not only **seductive** in
taste and texture, but can **ease
depression** as well.

---

mint leaves • champagne • spring water

Turn a deaf ear

Ignore the alarm on the next frosty
morning, and **relish** an extra hour of
peace before taking on the day.

---

considerate bosses • Beethoven

Finger your sockets

Discover unexpected pleasure in a two-minute massage of your eye sockets. Using two fingertips in a circular motion just beneath your brow, you'll access a range of pleasurable, relaxing acupressure points.

---

giggles • manicures • taking time

Relax and enjoy it

**Accept small pleasures as they
happen.** So much effort goes
into trying to influence the way
things happen, and so little is spent
in actually appreciating them.

---

thank yous • roasting coffee • pets

Give yourself a frill

Add excitement to your day by
wearing exotic underwear beneath
your everyday work clothes.

_____

orchids • wealth • dressing up • secrets

Make the first move

Good things generally happen
when someone makes them happen.

---

warm smiles • true love • special looks

See yellow

Contemplate the simple charm
and majesty of a giant sunflower
and **see the beauty** that Vincent
Van Gogh saw.

---

sun showers • falling leaves • full moons

Be licked

Submit yourself to the joyous
reaction of your dog after you've been
away for a couple of weeks.

---

coming home • delight • touching

Have fun

Meditate on the pleasure-building
wisdom of the immortal Guru Adrian:
'having fun is half the fun'.

---

skinny dipping • delight • hugs

Grant yourself a wish

Look heavenward ... note a falling
star (there's one every four minutes),
then **make a passionate wish** that
you know will come true.

---

payday • winning streaks • losing weight

Grin and bear it

Smile, and **instantly feel better.**
Smiling stimulates the pleasure
centre of your brain.

---

kisses • facials • free time • free love

Seek justice in a shop

Think **how delighted you'll feel**
when you find the garment
you've searched for all year —
on sale at half price.

---

untold wealth • leather upholstery

Hmmmm

Hum just one tune you associate
with **happy memories** of your
childhood, and **those good feelings
will come flooding back.**

---

snowflakes • carousels • Miss Piggy

Inhale a storm

Breathe in the cool, charged air
preceding a thunderstorm and
be refreshed by the magic,
mood-enhancing negative ions.
(Alternatively buy an ionizer for
the same effect.)

---

spring • cool breezes • rockpools

Make love to a tree

Trees **radiate positive feelings**.
Choose one that's a pleasure to be
near, then use it as a place to visit
when you want to **feel uplifted**.

---

home-grown • generosity • mountain tops

Write a love letter

(preferably to someone you know)

---

touches • tears of joy • making up

Lay back and listen

Listen to the monotonous sound
of rain on the roof as it **lulls you
back to a lazy, carefree sleep.**

---

completed tasks • Debussy • birdsongs

Turn off the TV

Rediscover the alternative pleasures
that life has to offer during
Prime Time.

---

hot showers • cello • children's laughter

First up

Remember how good it felt as a
child, being the **first one** to rise and
go outside on a frosty Sunday
morning.

---

sunrise • birthdays • fairy godmothers

Start the weekend early

For a few moments at the start of every working day **pretend it's a Saturday.** Carry that relaxed feeling with you throughout the day.

---

invitations • dancing • leisure

E =

Bolster your confidence with the
consolation that Albert Einstein didn't
talk until he was four years old,
and later failed both maths and physics.
(And Walt Disney was told he didn't
have a creative bone in his body.)

---

nature • good ideas • creative urges

Shower with a friend

Kiss a friend (or a complete stranger)
under a waterfall.

---

chilled wine • mountain streams • surf

Go solo

Indulge yourself with a slow,
do-it-yourself massage: oiling limb
by limb, part by part, until you
pleasure your entire body.
It takes thirty minutes.

---

aromatherapy • cuddles • sensuousness

Resign your maturity

**Become as spontaneous and as
contented as a child** by substituting
a few childlike qualities – even
superficial ones – for some of your
'adultness'.

---

angels • picnics • clover • cuddly toys

Spare a thought

Think one thought that would help
make the world a better place
and imagine it floating off into the
ether – **to be enjoyed** or discovered
by people unknown.

---

someone to come home to • joy

Go troppo

Slowly inhale the night air for the mysterious, sensual scent of frangipani.

---

bare skin • palm trees • love • Tahiti

Make your day

Close your eyes and **imagine waking
up to a perfect day**: the sun is
shining, the birds are singing,
and it's Sunday.

Chopin's Nocturnes • schmalzy songs

Live for the moment

Focus on every detail of every
moment – savouring every taste,
absorbing every sound, sensing
every colour – and you will **discover
pleasure** in things you might never
have known existed.

---

geranium window pots • waterfalls

Linger longer

At least once a day **take your time**
over something that **gives you
pleasure** ... dwell on it,
linger.

---

good books • old friends • sleeping late

Nude faces

Feel flesh like you've never felt it
before in the moments after
shaving a beard off.

---

cherubs • warm beds • open fires

Hang with the happy

Absorb the happiness that others
enjoy; spend more time with
happy people and you'll discover
happiness is catching.

---

taking time • convertibles • surprises

Take just one step

The most important step in enjoying
yourself is the first one — simply
making the effort to **enjoy yourself**.

---

soft focus • life • letters from friends

Clone your happiness

Summon up pleasures from your past, re-experience them in detail — what you saw, what you heard, how you felt. Then tap into that feeling whenever the need arises.

---

down pillows • silk pyjamas • hot bread

Face a towel

Feel the tension drain from your body
as you **lie back and drowse** under
a hot face towel.

---

problems solved • rest • good company

Think about love

Imagine **what a thrill it is** to learn
the person you've been admiring is
wildly in love with you. (Deep
thoughts of love can also arouse the
same physiological state as
meditation.)

---

erotic dreams • *Jimmy Stewart* • *calm*

Whirl

Abandon yourself in a dervish-like
dance while imagining yourself as
a participant in a primitive
tribal ritual.

Irish dancing • give in and enjoy it

Breathe in the surf

Listen to the lazy sound of a lapping
surf as it urges you to **slow down**
your breathing and your
pulse to match.

---

days off • tropical fruit • being alive

Ease down on a queen

Feel the relief as you sink into a queen-size mattress after a strenuous day on your feet.

---

opera in bed • obedient children • poetry

Be seduced by a romantic

Lose yourself for thirty intoxicating minutes by staring at any single painting from the Romantic period (1825–1900). Think what it was like to be there, seeing what the painter was seeing.

---

first loves • string quartets • tear jerkers

Complete anything

Feel the pleasure and satisfaction
that comes from completing a task
performed to the very best
of your abilities.

being first • compliments • good results

Tap your face

Feel a warm glow flow through your body as, slightly bent at the waist, you lightly pat your face with the fingers of each hand. This stimulates vital blood vessels and acupressure points in the facial area.

---

butterfly kisses • float tanks • rainbows

Be kind to dumb animals

Be thankful that animals aren't dumb:
treat them even passably well,
and they will be convinced **you're the
most wonderful being** ever created.
All that unquestioning positiveness
will make you **feel fantastic**.

---

newborn babies • reindeer • puppies

Play

Go on, **treat yourself** to a brand
new toy.

---

gifts • roller blades • mountain bikes

Bare to the breeze

Try standing naked and spread-eagled
in a brisk wind, allowing it to **caress
you** in ways that are decidedly
natural.

---

pink clouds • your picture in the paper

Tell a postman

Tell the postman or woman
what a great job they're doing.
You'll find the **good feelings** that
flow from it will be as much
yours as theirs.

---

favours • good news • free tickets

Repeat:

I feel complete harmony and contentment within myself. I radiate this feeling to all around me.

---

sunbeams • friends • spring showers

Concentrate on blissfulness

Concentrate on a single delight:
a sound, an image, an experience or
concept – until your mind is filled
with it – and **you are well on the way
to experiencing the pleasure of it.**

---

blue skies • candlelight • contentedness

Waste time dreaming

It is no waste of time to
daydream about pleasurable events:
seeing, hearing and feeling the things
that give you pleasure.

---

jackpots • promotion • perfection

Watch over an innocent

Recapture the beauty of your own
lost innocence as you watch
a child sleep.

---

mother of pearl • baby noises • bunnies

Throw a leg over

Get pleasure while you **do yourself good** by hiring a bicycle for a ride around the park.

---

fun parks • fresh fruit • Saturdays

Look through a vase

Nature specialises in enhancing life.
A vase of colourful flowers – or a
flowering pot plant – will help you
share this powerful feeling.

---

daisies • surprise parties • kind hearts

Bestow an award

Give yourself an award that **you really deserve** (best mother, best lover, best worker ...).

_____

passed exams • prizes • gratitude

Fix on delight

Concentrate on becoming happy;
make an effort to **have happy
thoughts**, and **your mood will lift**
accordingly.

---

daring backlines • shooting stars

Inject a positive

Talk yourself into feeling good by using positive words. Instead of 'fine', say '**happy**'; instead of 'okay', say '**wonderful**'; instead of 'all right', say '**excellent**'.

sound health • peace of mind • winning

Hop into hops

It's worth cultivating the taste,
because as millions will tell you,
there's nothing so pleasurable as a
cold beer on a warm day.

---

outdoor cafés • margaritas • long glasses

Live life

Search for the positive, humorous,
entertaining or even ridiculous
aspects of what you do — and **life
will seem lighter** as a result.

---

hot romance • warm baths • cool music

Stroke your cranium

Discover the intense pleasure
to be had from slowly stroking your
scalp from the forehead to the back
of the neck. Use all the fingertips.
Keep doing it until you **feel
your pulse slow.**

---

tender touches • massage • warm hands

Soak in sandalwood

Add a few drops of sandalwood or
chamomile oils to a warm bath, turn
down the lights, and **float away**.

---

azure seas • sunshine • basil • paradise

Guilt-free chocolate

Your appetite was right: chocolate
really does make you **feel calmer**
and more euphoric. (It boosts your
brain's production of serotonin,
the 'feel good' neurochemical.)

---

chocolate mousse • florentines

Think cool

Enjoy the pleasure of being cool
in steamy weather by standing rock
still and immersing yourself
in cool thoughts.

---

fame • ferns • being a kid • cold lager

Dress up your pleasures

Bring a touch of the exotic to your
day by dressing in formal wear —
just for the hell of it.

---

lucky breaks • balloons • emeralds

Get more out of your purse

Remember what Victor Hugo said:
'as the purse is emptied **the heart is
filled**'. He was right.

---

privileges • devotion • feeling secure

Find your levity

You'll always **feel on top of the world** if you can see the humour in the things other people find humorous about you.

---

fun fairs • convex mirrors • laughter

Get your name right

Can you **imagine how good it feels**
when someone you admire – who
you were barely introduced to months
ago – remembers your name
the very first time?

---

secret lovers • admiration • afterplay

Take a picture of yourself

Form a mental picture of
yourself – **happy, smiling and
enthusiastic** – and refer back to it
time and time again throughout
the day.

---

happy endings • boundless energy

Caress a toe

Ease yourself into a blissful state
of relaxation by applying a gentle
squeeze to the tip of each toe,
then beneath each toe where it joins
the foot – the power of reflexology
is at hand.

---

new socks • reflexology • thick carpets

Simplify

Approach life with your full attention
and an open mind, and you'll **find
pleasure in the most unlikely
places**: a baby's laugh, a perfect cloud,
a home-grown tomato, a wildflower,
or a breath of fresh air.

---

bonuses • campfires • lamb's wool

Be good now

Feel immediately uplifted the
moment you **indulge yourself** in an
act of altruism.

---

special favours • tenderness • heroes

Giggle

Giggling and laughing are known as
aerobics for the inside. Find
something to laugh about and **you'll
feel better immediately.**

---

jelly beans • children's books • gelato

Get sticky

Sip the best quality sticky dessert wine you can afford. Don't wait for dessert.

---

silk sheets • birthday wishes • serenity

Surprise the sun

The most pleasant and creative
moment of the day is just before the
sun rises; try it, with no other
purpose but **pleasure in mind.**

---

virgin sand • virgin olive oil • surprises

Go to the temples

Massage your temples with a mixture
of clary sage, geranium and jasmine
in a bland carrier oil (such as
sweet almond). **It's as agreeable as
it is relaxing**.

---

good horoscopes • rainforests • pearls

Bow before beauty

Take a moment to **clear your mind**
before assessing an object of beauty.
Then absorb it as if you've never
witnessed such an object before.

---

radiance • crystals • Ansel Adams

Give thanks to worms

Wear good quality silk next to your skin and **every movement becomes an act of pleasure.**

new car smell • fresh snow • shopping

Keep your mouth shut

Communicate with somebody important (to you) without uttering a word.

---

guardian angels • freedom of choice

Be positive

Be positive that you can **bring out
the best in life**, just by your frame
of mind.

---

respect • going home • financial success

Think about gold

Ponder **how satisfying it is** ...
to celebrate your golden wedding
anniversary, absolutely certain **you
made the right decision** fifty
years ago.

---

generous friends • pastel colours

See red

Remember the thrill of that little glimpse of red suit you saw leaving the room all those Christmas Eves ago?

---

loving parents • presents • certainty

Tug your lobe

Excite the rest of your body by
gently pinching then stretching your
ear lobes, before massaging your ears
all over. There are dozens of
influential acupressure points in
and around this area.

---

long friendship • bubble baths

Get high

Discover the pleasure to be had at high altitudes when you stand at the top of a mountain, quietly looking down on the splendour below. (Every vista is splendid when viewed from great heights.)

---

art deco • Fifth Avenue • setting sun

Get into slow mastication

Savour every bite: the slower you eat,
the more enjoyment and satisfaction
you derive from your food.

---

freshly-baked bread • olive groves

Reach for a hug

Give yourself pleasure at the same time as you bestow it, with a simple hug.

---

lilies • Romeo & Juliet • essential oils

Get a buzz today

You'll **immediately get more out of life** if you **make believe** you're loving it, you can't get enough of it, and that you're familiar with this feeling.

---

showing pleasure • sunrise • extra time

Air your lungs

Fill yourself with uninhibited
pleasure by screaming at the top of
your lungs as you drive with the top
down and the wind in your hair.

---

good help • mountain roads • outdoors

Savour lightness

Make your happiness last longer by feasting on light, raw and easily digested foods. (Heavy or convenience foods deflate the mood.)

---

spearmint • crisp salads • mushrooms

Follow many routes

As there is no single course to
happiness, you'll find **the path is
more pleasurable** if you try a number
of smaller ways throughout the day.

---

rising late • sincerity • kittens

Follicles fondled

Stimulate any number of pleasurable
little acupressure points on your
skull by having your hair brushed –
slowly and protractedly.

---

cat naps • quiet • passionate kisses

Create

Paint, play, sculpt, write,
dance ... to **create** anything is one of
the greatest pleasures of all.

---

surprise embraces • baking cakes

Read about yourself

Think **how sweet** it is to open the
paper and see your smiling picture
with a positive caption beneath.
(Carry this imagined picture with you
for the rest of the day.)

---

homecomings • flattering portraits

Make someone else's day

There is no better way to **enrich your own life**, than to **help someone else** enrich theirs. Be generous – for the pleasure of it.

---

confidants • pay rises • tranquillity

Audit your joy

Make an effort to **appreciate the positive** aspects of your life as it is now. Treasure what you've got and you can **count on much more**.

---

sea breezes • guilt-free pleasure

Extend your holidays

Pretend you're on holiday today:
do little things that amplify this
impression, and **watch your day
become brighter**.

love-making • shady porches • seagulls

Take the whole day

Dedicate a day to just being
with someone you **love, without
distraction** or expectation.

---

vineyards • true love • togetherness

Use your nose

Get twice the pleasure from smelling
flowers such as lavender or rose.
(Their scents stimulate the
production of the relaxing chemical,
serotonin, in the brain.)

---

celebration • ocean drives • bouquets

Stay for breakfast

One day each week, **treat yourself**
to breakfast in bed, armed with a
newspaper and nothing to
do for an hour.

---

café latte • Sunday • time to spare

Go for the jocular

Look for the amusing side to life.
When you see it you'll **find pleasure**
as well as amusement.

---

carnivals • bare feet • comic moments

Pack the flax

Discover pleasure as well as
relaxation by lying back with a tiny
silk pillow of flax seeds (linseeds)
covering your eyes.

---

restful moments • accomplishment

Get warm and friendly

The most pleasurable heating system
ever devised is when you **cuddle a
friendly warm body** on your side
of the bed.

---

double rainbows • goosebumps • caresses

Warble

Choose any song in a major key,
sing it loudly and enthusiastically,
and **you'll feel better** and have
forgotten your blues by the end
of the 36th bar.

---

rousing anthems • heavenly voices

Ginseng and be merry

Ginseng is renowned for its ability to **excite** the nervous system at the same time as it relaxes it. This may be why it's so sought after as an aphrodisiac.

---

starry skies • fresh air • outdoor eating

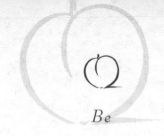

Be

Rejoice in being. At the end of your
days, when you reflect on your life,
there will be no moment more
important than this very instant.

---

still lakes • your name in lights